the

social success
workbook for teens

skill-building activities for teens
with **nonverbal learning** disorder,
asperger's disorder & other
social-skill problems

BARBARA COOPER, MPS
NANCY WIDDOWS, MS

Instant Help Books
A Division of New Harbinger Publications, Inc.

Distributed in Canada by Raincoast Books

Copyright © 2008 by Barbara Cooper and Nancy Widdows
Instant Help Books
A Division of New Harbinger Publications, Inc.
5674 Shattuck Avenue
Oakland, CA 94609
www.newharbinger.com

Cover design by Amy Shoup
Illustrations by Julie Olson

Printed in the United States of America

FSC
Mixed Sources
Product group from well-managed forests and other controlled sources
Cert no. SW-COC-002283
www.fsc.org
© 1996 Forest Stewardship Council

Library of Congress Cataloging-in-Publication Data

Cooper, Barbara, 1953-
  The social success workbook for teens : skill-building activities for teens with nonverbal learning disorder, Asperger's disorder, and other social-skill problems / Barbara Cooper and Nancy Widdows.
    p. cm.
  ISBN-13: 978-1-57224-614-0 (pbk. : alk. paper)
  ISBN-10: 1-57224-614-6 (pbk. : alk. paper) 1. Developmental disabilities. 2. Social skills in adolescence. I. Widdows, Nancy. II. Title.
  RJ506.D47C66 2008
  618.92'8588--dc22
                          2008016241

10   09   08

10   9   8   7   6   5   4   3   2

We dedicate this book to the many SuperKids who trusted us enough to share their struggles and successes and who taught us so much in the process. Special thanks to Larry B. for taking the time to share his wisdom.

—Barbara Cooper and Nancy Widdows

contents

✳ contents

introduction

Dear Reader,

This book presents activities to help you understand and strengthen your social skills and achieve a level of social comfort. When you can better understand yourself, your emotions, the emotions and responses of other people, and how the social world works, it becomes easier for you to handle the challenges you face. Everyone can benefit from strengthening these skills.

Over the years, we have had the opportunity to help lots of children and teens learn more about themselves and their social-skill levels, and we have helped them recognize and use their strengths to compensate for and overcome their weaknesses. It has been amazing and inspiring to watch kids grow and become more comfortable with themselves and their places in the social world. We are excited to offer you information and activities that have helped those kids. All the kids we have worked with over the years have taught us so much about what helps them and what doesn't, so we present this material to you with respect for your views and a real desire to help you.

The activities in this book are arranged in order and build upon one another. There are some activities that we suggest you do with a trusted adult. These activities require you to evaluate your own abilities, and we know that can be difficult. You may want to ask for feedback once you've completed any activity; getting someone else's perspective when it comes to social skills is almost always helpful.

We know this work can be challenging. It takes courage and energy, and it pays off! Our hope is that you accept this challenge to find your place in the world.

—Nancy and Barbara

comic-strip stories

you need to know

If you want to know what other people are feeling in a certain situation, look at everything that has just happened (the context) and at their faces and bodies for clues.

Max can't find his book report project, and it's due the next day. His brother Tommy sees him frantically searching the house, looking for it. When Tommy asks Max where his video game is, Max starts to scream and kick Tommy. Normally, Tommy's reaction would be to scream back. This time, however, Tommy was able to understand that Max was frustrated about his project and was actually venting his own anger.

directions

To practice tuning in to what someone else might be feeling, look at the situations below and write a story about how the kids are feeling. Remember to take into consideration the sequence of events and actions, the setting, and facial and body cues.

_____

_____

_____

_____

_____

_____

_____

_____

take note

Write a few sentences about a time when you noticed someone feeling frustrated.

_____

_____

_____

Could you tell that this person was frustrated by what was happening or by looking for facial expressions and body language, or both? _____

Write a few sentences about a time when you noticed someone feeling annoyed.

_____

_____

_____

Could you tell that this person was annoyed by what was happening or by looking for facial expressions and body language, or both? _____

Write a few sentences about a time when you noticed someone feeling excited.

_____

_____

_____

Could you tell that this person was excited by what was happening or by looking for facial expressions and body language, or both? _____

Write a few sentences about a time when you noticed someone feeling bored.

_____

_____

_____

Could you tell that this person was bored by what was happening or by looking for facial expressions and body language, or both? _____

things that make me happy 2

you need to know

Learning more about your own feelings can help you understand yourself. What makes you happy might be different from what makes other people happy. It's important to know what makes you happy so that you can let other people know. Sometimes that helps other people give you what you need or want.

When Carl got home from school, his body was tired. His mind was racing with all the thoughts of what had gone on in school during the day. Carl's mom believed that Carl should get his homework and chores done right after school so that he could relax later in the evening. When Carl was younger, he followed his mom's plan. If he wanted to take a break when he got home from school, he would have to fight with his mother about doing his homework later. Now that Carl is older, he thinks that taking a break after school and doing his homework and chores later would make him happy. He told his mom that he wanted to try this new schedule. Carl's mom agreed to let him try it and saw that he was able to manage his time very well and that he was calmer and happier all evening.

directions

On this page, create a collage, drawing, poem, or story about things that make you happy.

take note

As you look at your creation, think about whom you would feel comfortable sharing it with. List those names here.

_____

_____

_____

Think about what other people can do to help you feel happier. What important person in your life could you share these thoughts with? What thoughts would you share?

_____

_____

_____

_____

_____

_____

_____

Do you have any friends who might list the same things if they were asked about what made them happy?

_____

_____

_____

3 things that make me worry

you need to know

Things that make you worry might be different from things that make other people worry. It's important to know what makes you worry so that you can communicate your anxiety to people who can help you learn ways to cope with, and reduce, your worries.

Amanda wanted to join the after-school drama club. Each time there was a meeting, Amanda thought about going, but she became so worried about going alone that she didn't go at all. When she missed these meetings, she ended up feeling bad about herself, regretting her decision. Amanda was able to tell her guidance counselor about it. Her guidance counselor knew another girl who was a member of the club. He introduced Amanda to this girl, who invited her to go to the next meeting together. That way, Amanda was able to overcome her anxiety about new situations.

directions

On this page, create a collage, drawing, poem, or story about things that worry you.

take note

As you look at your creation, think about whom you would feel comfortable sharing it with. List those names here.

_____

_____

_____

Think about what other people can do to help you feel less anxious. What important person in your life could you share these thoughts with? What thoughts would you share?

_____

_____

_____

_____

_____

Ask these people to help you come up with strategies for coping with your worries and anxieties. Write some of these strategies below.

_____

_____

_____

_____

_____

things that make me angry 4

you need to know

Things that make you angry might be different from things that make other people angry. It's important to know what makes you angry so that you can communicate your anger to people who can help you learn ways to safely express and manage your anger.

Chris was at home in his room, reading a book. His brother Jack was listening to music in his own room. Chris had a hard time concentrating on the book while the music was playing. He became angry, thinking that his brother should know how much loud music bothered him. Suddenly, he went into Jack's room and screamed at him to lower the volume. Startled and upset at Chris's angry outburst, Jack refused. Later, when Chris and Jack talked about it with their parents, it became apparent that Jack had no idea his music was bothering Chris. Chris had assumed that Jack would know that music played at that level bothered him. In fact, their mom had been in the house at the time, and she thought the volume of the music was fine.

directions

On this page, create a collage, drawing, poem, or story about things that make you angry.

take note

As you look at your "things that make me angry" page, is there anything that you didn't realize made you angry? If so, what?

_____

_____

_____

As you look at your creation, think about whom you would feel comfortable sharing it with. List those names here.

_____

_____

_____

Think about what other people can do to help you manage your anger so that you can express it safely. What important person in your life could you share these thoughts with? What thoughts would you share?

_____

_____

_____

_____

Ask these people to help you come up with strategies for coping with your anger. Write some of these strategies here. (There are suggested strategies in activities later in this book.)

_____

_____

_____

_____

5   shades of anger

you need to know

Anger has many shades. You may feel mildly annoyed, mad, very angry, furious, or full of rage. Some people are quick to get angry, and their anger may be out of proportion to the event that triggers it. Usually that happens because their anger has been building over a long period of time. If people do not know how to express their anger when it is first triggered, it can build up like a volcano and explode all at once. Often the explosion happens over something that seems small.

Being aware of the shades of anger can help you know what level of anger you are feeling at the time you first feel it. It is an important first step in being able to safely express and manage your anger before it builds up and you explode.

Every time George went to his science class, John and his group of friends would trip, poke, and tease him—but only if there were no adults around. When adults were looking, the boys pretended to be George's friends. Although George tried to ignore them, they didn't stop, and his anger slowly built up. One evening at home, George's mom asked if he had finished his homework. He picked up a heavy textbook, threw it onto the floor, and began to scream. George's mom was confused about what had caused this outburst. She thought she was asking George an everyday question and couldn't understand why he had gotten so upset.

George's mom waited until he calmed down and kindly asked him some questions about how life was going for him. George was able to share what was happening in science class, even though he hated talking about it. Together they were able to come up with strategies to help George deal with upsetting experiences and address them when they happened.

directions

In the space below, draw scenarios that show different shades of anger.

1. Show a scenario of something that makes you mildly annoyed.

2. Show a scenario of something that makes you mad.

3. Show a scenario of something that makes you very angry.

4. Show a scenario of something that makes you absolutely furious.

take note

Looking back at scenario 1, write what you think would be a safe way to express and manage feeling annoyed in that situation.

_____

_____

_____

Looking back at scenario 2, write what you think would be a safe way to express and manage feeling mad in that situation.

_____

_____

_____

Looking back at scenario 3, write what you think would be a safe way to express and manage feeling very angry in that situation.

_____

_____

_____

Looking back at scenario 4, write what you think would be a safe way to express and manage feeling furious in that situation.

_____

_____

_____

As your anger becomes more intense, does it get harder to think about expressing and managing your feelings? If so, at what point, or shade of anger, does it become too difficult?

_____

_____

where do I feel these feelings?

Sue went to Amy's house, thinking they were going to play Amy's new video game. When Sue arrived, Amy said that she was already tired of playing the game and that they were going to do something else. Sue felt herself breathing faster than normal. She felt warm and she found herself clenching and unclenching her hands, which had formed fists. Sue knew these signals meant she was beginning to feel angry. She also knew that if time went by and she tried to ignore her feelings, once she became angry she would have difficulty getting over it. Sue was able to do these things:

- Acknowledge to herself that she was disappointed, and even angry, about the change in plans

- Begin to slow her breathing down and shake out her hands

- Think about other good times she had had with Amy and tell herself that they could have fun doing something else

directions

For each outline below, think about something that makes you feel the way that body is labeled. Stand and make your body into the position that you take when you have this feeling. Color the areas inside the outline where you feel this feeling the most. For example, if you ball your hands into fists when you are angry, color in the hands of the outline labeled "Angry."

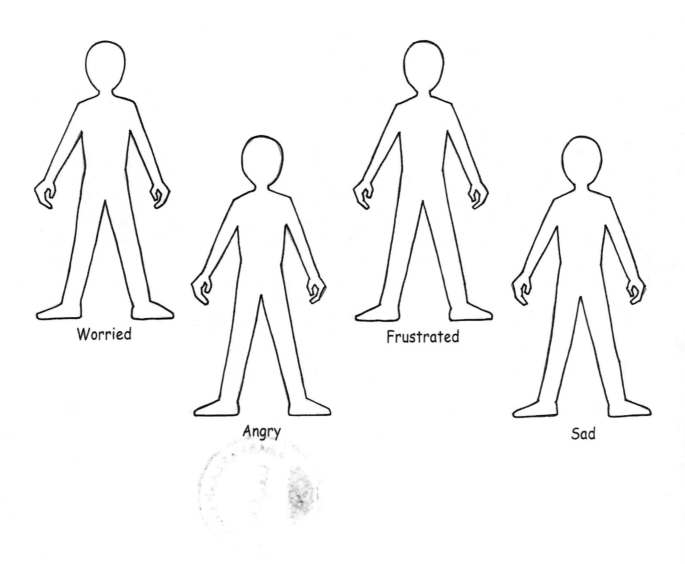

Worried

Frustrated

Angry

Sad

take note

Now that you've colored in the outlines, answer these questions:

Where in your body do you feel:

anger? _____

frustration? _____

worry? _____

sadness? _____

Do you think you notice these feelings in your body when they are happening?

☐ Yes ☐ No

If yes, it might be helpful to talk with someone you trust when you are feeling that way. You can also use some cool-down tools that you will explore in activities later in this book.

If no, it might be helpful for you and family members to talk about what you feel like inside when you are having strong feelings so that you can become aware of how your face and body look. Members of your family can help you practice tuning in to your feelings. When you know how you feel, you can use the coping strategies you are learning so that you can deal with these feelings in an okay way.

7 paint-chip key chain

you need to know

Some people are really good at knowing what they are feeling, and some people need to learn how to tune in to how they feel. The paint-chip key chain is a tool to help you know what you are feeling at a particular time.

Jamie was having a hard time at school. She didn't really know why, but right before gym class she would get a little upset. If anyone asked her if something was wrong, she would get angry. When the gym teacher asked her to explain why she wouldn't participate, Jamie just didn't know what to say. She was confused and upset.

Her school counselor knew that Jamie learned better when people explained things to her using pictures instead of just words. Her counselor knew that using colors to match feelings might help Jamie know what she was feeling. Together they made a paint-chip key chain. Jamie practiced using it at home and in school when she wasn't upset. That taught her to pay attention to what she was feeling when things were okay. When she got upset before gym one day, she took out the key chain and really thought about what she was feeling. She picked the color chip for "worried." When her teacher asked her why she was worried, Jamie was able to explain that she didn't like gym because she was clumsy. She felt inferior and humiliated when she had to participate. Her teacher was then able to offer Jamie alternative activities in gym that helped her feel less worried.

directions

How to Make Your Paint-Chip Key Chain

Have someone take you to a hardware store so that you can pick out at least fifteen paint-chip samples in a variety of colors. Make sure you have at least one shade of blue, red, yellow, orange, green, purple, white, and black.

1. Pick a paint-chip color for each of the following feelings: happy, sad, angry, frustrated, scared, worried, excited, lonely, overwhelmed, surprised, calm, and shy. You can add any other feelings that you think you feel a lot.

2. Cut each paint-chip into a small square or rectangle and, using a hole puncher, place a hole in one corner. Label the back of each chip with the feeling for which you chose that color.

3. Using a key ring or piece of string, connect the chips.

How to Use Your Paint-Chip Key Chain

1. Carry the key chain in your pocket so that you have it with you at all times. Experiment with using it at different times.

2. When you have any type of strong feeling, take the key chain out and find the paint chip that best matches what you are feeling. Notice how your body is feeling at that time. For example, some people make tights fists when they are angry or jiggle their legs when they are worried.

3. Even when you are not having a strong feeling, take the key chain out occasionally and find the paint chip that best matches your feeling. Again, notice how your body is feeling at that time.

4. When you are confused about how you are feeling, take the key chain out and find the chip that best describes what you might be feeling. Remember that it's possible to have two different feelings at the same time; that may be what's confusing you.

Practice using the paint-chip key chain, and see if you get better at knowing and paying attention to what you are feeling. If there is an adult who can practice with you at home, it would be good for them to use the key chain too so that you can notice what other people look like when they have a particular feeling.

take note

Write about a time when you used your key chain. What happened?

_____

_____

_____

_____

_____

_____

_____

When do you think using the key chain might be helpful to you?

_____

_____

List some situations where you are confused about your feelings.

_____

_____

_____

_____

_____

different points of view 8

you need to know

People who spend time together can have different thoughts and feelings about what happens when they are together. It's important to know that other people might have a different way of seeing what's going on.

Spencer was playing chess with Bobby. Spencer had played chess only a few times before, while Bobby was a member of his school's chess club and was quite good at it. Halfway through the game, when Spencer was stuck and unable to make a move, Bobby offered to help by teaching Spencer some strategies that he thought Spencer didn't know. Spencer was frustrated. He became angry when Bobby tried to help, thinking that Bobby was really trying to tell Spencer to make a bad move so that he could win. Bobby got upset because he just wanted to help. He didn't like to be accused of cheating.

Even though Spencer and Bobby were together, they were having different thoughts and feelings about what was happening.

directions

Draw something that happened to you today when you were with other kids that might have involved one of these feelings: frustration, excitement, disappointment, hope, worry, loneliness, or exclusion.

What do you think the other kids might have been feeling? Draw a picture to describe it.

take note

Write about your first drawing. Include what happened and how you felt.

_____

_____

_____

_____

_____

_____

_____

Write about your second drawing. Tell how the other people might have felt.

_____

_____

_____

_____

_____

_____

_____

Share these drawings and what you wrote with an adult you trust. If you are having misperceptions about experiences with other kids, people you trust may be able to help you to see things from other points of view.

9 something about myself I'll never change and something I'd like to change

you need to know
We all have many parts to who we are. Everyone is really good at some things and not so good at others. Thinking about your strengths and weaknesses will help you know that you are good at some things even while you are working on getting better at what's hard for you.

Justin is really great at using a computer. He knows more about computers than most other kids. He is great at helping kids at school with their computer problems, and he is proud of being able to do it. It's a part of himself that he would never change.

When it's time for lunch, Justin has trouble finding other kids to hang out with. He wanders around the school alone. He feels lonely and frustrated that other kids don't seem to like to be with him. Justin is not so great at connecting with other kids. It's something he would love to change.

directions

Draw a picture or write about something that you really like about yourself and would never want to change.

Draw a picture or write about something about yourself that you don't like and wish you could change.

take note

What aspect of yourself did you draw or write about that you would never want to change?

_____

Why? _____

_____

_____

What aspect of yourself did you draw or write about that you would like to change?

_____

Why? _____

_____

_____

What aspect of yourself do you think your parents would like you to change?

_____

Why? _____

_____

_____

Share your drawings or writing with an adult you trust. This person may be able to help you find ways to work on what you'd like to change.

what's different about my brain? 10

you need to know

People who have difficulty with social skills often have parts of their brains that don't exactly do what they're supposed to do. It may be difficult for them to know what others are thinking and feeling because their brains aren't helping them know how to take in this information and use it. People who can do that easily can look at other people's facial expressions and body language and get lots of information that they use to help them get along with other people. This skill is often referred to as "reading social cues."

It is difficult to make friends and get along easily with other people when you have trouble reading social cues. Scientists have learned that other parts of the brain can do the work of the parts that don't work so well. In order to make that happen, it's necessary to practice what is difficult for you by learning how to read social cues. That can be accomplished in many ways: by having adults in your life who can help you, by being in social-skills programs in and out of school— and by using this workbook! What is most important is that you understand why it may be so hard for you to do things that come so easily to other people and, know that you can help yourself become better at social skills.

Randi and Jessica went to meet Angela during their lunch period. Angela was sitting at their usual table, looking upset. Her eyes were looking down, her mouth was frowning, and she was holding her head in her hands. Jessica knew, by noticing these cues, that Angela was upset. As they approached Angela, Randi, who didn't notice these things, started to talk about a TV show she had seen the night before. Jessica asked Randi to stop so she could check with Angela and find out what was wrong. Angela proceeded to talk only to Jessica about what was upsetting her. Randi felt ignored and didn't know why Angela would do that to her. Later, Jessica was able to tell Randi that Angela was upset and thought Randi was insensitive and uncaring because she didn't pay attention to Angela's social cues (how upset her face looked).

directions

Think about your strengths and weaknesses. What are you great at? What do you have trouble with? Below, create a list of strengths and weaknesses so that you can begin to know more about how your particular brain works.

Strengths	Weaknesses

take note

One purpose of this workbook is to get better at understanding yourself so you can know what you need to learn to increase your social skills. When someone has trouble reading the social cues of others, they might also have trouble knowing their own strengths and weaknesses.

Share the list you just made with an adult you trust. That adult may be able to help you see strengths and weaknesses you may not be aware of.

How do these strengths and weaknesses affect your relationships with other people?

_____

_____

_____

_____

_____

_____

_____

_____

_____

_____

_____

_____

_____

_____

11 feelings checklist

you need to know

To continue working on your social skills, practice paying attention to your feelings. Some people have a hard time knowing what they felt during their day, which makes it difficult for them to communicate this information to other people. Others can identify what they felt when something bad happened, but they don't want to talk about difficult feelings after the fact because it just seems to bring those bad feelings back.

It's important to be able to let your parents or other important people know how you felt when they were not around. When kids don't tell parents or other important people what's happened, their feelings can build up inside until one day, without even expecting it, they explode.

This checklist can help you tell your parents and other important people what you have felt during your day. It is good practice to help you pay attention to your feelings.

directions

Circle the phrase that best describes how often you felt the following today:

Happy	not at all	a little	a lot	all the time
Surprised	not at all	a little	a lot	all the time
Sad	not at all	a little	a lot	all the time
Worried	not at all	a little	a lot	all the time
Frustrated	not at all	a little	a lot	all the time
Lonely	not at all	a little	a lot	all the time
Included	not at all	a little	a lot	all the time
Angry	not at all	a little	a lot	all the time
Left out	not at all	a little	a lot	all the time
Different	not at all	a little	a lot	all the time
Shy	not at all	a little	a lot	all the time
Hurt	not at all	a little	a lot	all the time
Hopeful	not at all	a little	a lot	all the time
Annoyed	not at all	a little	a lot	all the time
Embarrassed	not at all	a little	a lot	all the time
I asked to join with others.	not at all	a little	a lot	all the time
I listened to others.	not at all	a little	a lot	all the time
I felt like hurting myself.	not at all	a little	a lot	all the time
I felt like hurting someone else.	not at all	a little	a lot	all the time
I felt very different at home than I did out in the world	not at all	a little	a lot	all the time

because _____.

I acted in ways I regretted	not at all	a little	a lot	all the time

when I _____.

I felt I had to ignore my feelings	not at all	a little	a lot	all the time

when _____.

take note

Did using the feelings checklist help you tell someone else about your day? Explain.

_____

_____

_____

After filling out a checklist at the end of a day, did any of your answers surprise you?

☐ Yes ☐ No

If yes, what surprised you?

_____

_____

_____

Would you do anything differently tomorrow because of how you felt about something today?

☐ Yes ☐ No

If yes, what would you do?

_____

_____

_____

Are there any feelings you would add to this checklist? If so, what are they?

_____

_____

_____

---

you need to know

Some people lose it when they are feeling overwhelmed, frustrated, angry, or very tired. Part of learning how to keep it together and to avoid losing it is to understand what happens inside you in stressful situations. Then you can choose to either avoid those situations, if possible, or learn to cool down when the stressful feelings begin. As you get older, that becomes easier to do.

Jake was playing a board game with two other boys. At one point in the game, there was a disagreement about the rules. The rules booklet was missing from the game, but Jake was absolutely sure that he knew the correct way to play. The other boys disagreed and said, "Majority rules. We are playing our way." Jake was extremely frustrated because he knew he was right. He put his fingers under the game board and turned it over while shouting at his friends. They asked Jake to calm down, but it was too late. Jake was melting down.

If Jake knew that accurate game rules were important to him, he could have discussed the rules before the game began since there might be different rule versions of the game. When he began to feel upset, Jake could also have reminded himself that people may disagree on the rules, and when that happens the disagreement is usually resolved by "majority rules." He could have told himself that he didn't like to play this way, but since he was happy to be playing a game with other kids, it was not worth getting upset. Jake could have taken a few deep breaths to cool down and reminded himself to choose friendship in this situation over rules.

directions

Before you can learn how to keep it together, you need to be able to identify situations that push your buttons or get you so upset that you lose it. This activity is designed to help you become aware of your boiling point so that you can come up with a way to tell yourself you're about to lose it. Then you can use a coping strategy that works for you. In activities to come, you will explore different coping strategies to find those that work for you.

List three things that overwhelm you. On a scale from 1 to 10, rate how much each overwhelms you.

1. _____

1	2	3	4	5	6	7	8	9	10
Calm			Annoyed			Angry			"Losing It"

2. _____

1	2	3	4	5	6	7	8	9	10
Calm			Annoyed			Angry			"Losing It"

3. _____

1	2	3	4	5	6	7	8	9	10
Calm			Annoyed			Angry			"Losing It"

Describe a time when you lost it: _____

_____

_____

What happened just before you lost it?* _____

_____

Can you identify what you felt? _____

_____

*If you have difficulty figuring out what's stressful for you, ask an adult you trust to help you. That adult may have a good idea of what causes you to lose it.

take note

Here are some strategies you can use when you realize you are approaching 5 on the overwhelmed scale:

- Tell yourself, "I'm approaching number 5."

- Take a deep breath and tell yourself, "There will be a big social cost if I lose it now."*

Depending on the situation, you can also try these things:

- Walk away from the situation.

- Find someone you trust that you can talk with about what just happened.

- Use the cool-down tools in activities 17-20.

Write your new ideas for how to keep it together:

_____

_____

_____

_____

_____

_____

_____

_____

_____

_____

_____

_____

_____

*The "social cost" refers to how other people will view you as you are losing it. It also refers to how you may feel about yourself after you've lost control.

13 when I am angry

you need to know

Some kids don't know why people get angry at them. They also might not know why they get angry at other people. Being aware of what you do to make others angry and what they do to make you angry can help you make and keep friends.

Story 1

Rachel is very concerned about school rules. She prides herself on following them very closely. She also pays attention to when her peers break those rules. One day, Rachel saw Katie in math class but then did not see her in Spanish class. Rachel told the Spanish teacher that Katie had been in math class. Katie got in trouble for skipping class. The next day, Katie was mean to Rachel in front of the whole class, and all the students laughed. Rachel didn't understand why everyone sided with Katie when all Rachel was doing was telling the truth. Rachel didn't know that telling on someone, especially when the situation doesn't concern her, gets people angry. (See activity 27.)

Story 2

Greg gets angry when his father asks him over and over again to take out the trash while Greg is playing his video game. Greg thinks his father should know that he is trying to beat a level he hadn't reached before in his game and how important that is to him. The third time his father interrupts him, insisting Greg do it now or the game will be taken away, Greg loses it and throws the game controller at his father, who takes away Greg's game privileges for a month.

directions

Draw a picture of something you do that makes other people angry.

Draw a picture of something other people do that makes you angry.

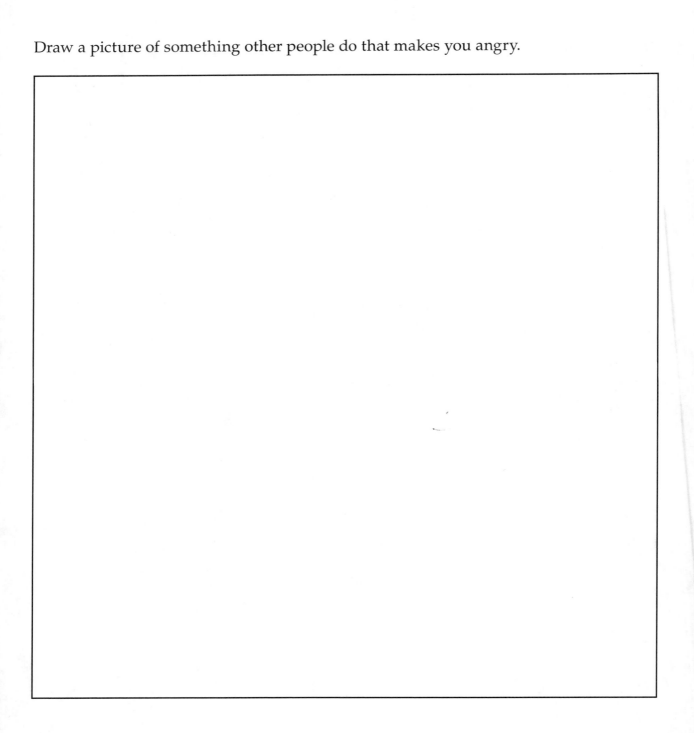

take note

For your first drawing:

How do other people feel or what do they think when they see you do what you drew about?

_____

_____

Do you think there is a way you could change what you do?   ☐ Yes ☐ No

If yes, what could you do differently so that others wouldn't be so mad at you?

_____

_____

For your second drawing:

Why do you think the people are doing what they are doing?

_____

_____

Are you able to let them know you are angry?   ☐ Yes ☐ No

If yes, how do you let them know?

_____

_____

14 when you pretend things don't bother you

you need to know

Sometimes people have unpleasant or upsetting experiences and don't know how to react to them. They may get upset at the time of the experience, but when it is over they try hard not to think about it or talk about it with anyone. They think doing that will make the unpleasant feelings go away.

What often happens is that those feelings don't go away but instead build up inside. Then one day when they experience something slightly upsetting, they lose it as if something major had happened.

Carmen was having a difficult week. In the lunchroom on Monday, she went over to the table of girls she usually sat with, and they told her she couldn't sit with them anymore. Every day, she had to roam the cafeteria with her tray to find a place to sit alone where she wouldn't be bothered. On Wednesday, she told her guidance counselor that everything was fine, even when the guidance counselor asked about lunchtime. On Thursday, Carmen's mother noticed that she seemed moody and asked if everything was okay. Carmen said it was. She really thought keeping her feelings to herself would make them go away, and she thought that if she talked about the feelings they would get worse. On Friday, someone in the lunchroom stepped in front of her in line. Carmen threw her tray to the floor and screamed at the girl, who hadn't even been aware that Carmen was in line.

directions

For the next three days, keep a log listing events that upset you. Write what happened, what "shade of anger" you felt (see activity 5) and some notes about any thoughts that may be stuck inside you. Drawing a picture may also be helpful.

If this activity is difficult for you, you may want to use the feelings checklist in activity 11 as a tool to help you tune in; then try the activity again. You may not want to keep this log, but learning to tune in is necessary for you to be able to gain control over losing it and keeping it together. Just spend a few minutes after school on it and plan to do something fun or relaxing when you are done, as a reward!

Day 1:

Event	Shade of Anger	Notes

Day 2:

Event	Shade of Anger	Notes

Day 3:

Event	Shade of Anger	Notes

take note

Was it easy for you to do this activity or difficult? Describe any thoughts or feelings you have about what you experienced.

_____

_____

_____

_____

How did you feel after you wrote about the difficult experiences you had during the day?

_____

_____

_____

_____

What did you do for yourself as a reward?

_____

_____

_____

If your reward wasn't good enough to help you let go of your difficult feelings, come up with a better one!

If you continue to practice, you can figure out if doing this activity helps you avoid the buildup of bad feelings over time that may cause you to lose it. The more you practice this strategy, the easier it will become and the easier you will find it to keep it together and feel more in control.

when plans change 15

you need to know

Some people have a hard time when they think something is going to happen in a certain way and then it doesn't go the way they thought it would. It is as if they had pictures in their heads and really want those pictures to become what happens. When things don't go your way, it's important to realize that plans change for many different reasons.

Every Tuesday, Adam attends the computer club at his school. He looks forward to Tuesdays because of it. One Tuesday, Adam goes to the club and no one is there. He goes to the school office only to find out that the meeting has been cancelled that day. The person in the office acts as if he should have known, since there was an announcement made that morning. Adam runs outside to find his bus and realizes it has already left.

directions

Below are some things that might happen next:

1. Adam feels anxious and angry and is unable to think of what to do next. He starts pacing back and forth, mumbling to himself. Kids standing around see him and quickly move away.

2. Adam takes a deep breath, goes back to the office, and asks to call his mom.

3. Adam tells himself that everything will be okay, goes to the school library, and does homework until the late bus arrives.

4. Adam becomes angry at the person in the office who told him the club meeting was cancelled. Feeling as if he wants to fix the situation so that it comes out the way he expected, he yells at her and demands that she open the club room so that he can work on the computer anyway.

Even though Adam is not getting to do what he thought he would be doing that day, which ending would be the best for him?

☐ 1   ☐ 2   ☐ 3   ☐ 4

Why did you choose the one you did?

_____

_____

_____

_____

_____

_____

_____

_____

take note

Write about a time at home when you couldn't change the plan in your head.

_____

_____

_____

_____

_____

_____

_____

_____

Write about a time at school when you couldn't change the plan in your head.

_____

_____

_____

_____

_____

_____

_____

_____

16 changing the plan in your head

you need to know

Sometimes creating a visual image of what you need to do to deal with unexpected events can help you change the plan in your head. Dealing with unexpected events in a calmer, less upsetting way will help you handle change and avoid losing it.

In the previous activity, Adam experienced a change of plan. Lots of people who find it really difficult when plans change either lose it or have a hard time focusing and thinking clearly about what to do next. One thing you can do is to think about changing the plan in your head. That can make it easier for you to handle unexpected events.

Look at the following picture. The next time something unexpected comes up and you have to change your plan, try to think of this picture and see if it will help you.

directions

Think about a time when something unexpected happened to you and you had to change your plan. Write what happened:

_____

_____

_____

_____

_____

_____

_____

_____

Now, using the "change the plan" drawing on page 50 as a guide, draw or write about yourself dealing with changing the plan in the situation above.

take note

Do you think you can remember this picture when something unexpected happens?

☐ Yes ☐ No

If yes, try it out. Write about what happened after you tried it.

_____

_____

_____

_____

_____

If no, you may want to copy either our picture or yours to keep with you to remember to use it. Another suggestion is for you to come up with a different way to remind yourself when you are stressed out that you need to change the plan. For some people, it's easier to remember a visual symbol than to think in words about what to do. What do you think could work for you?

_____

_____

_____

_____

_____

_____

_____

you need to know

A cool-down tool is something you can use to calm yourself. Many people think that when they are upset, there's nothing that can help, but we know that there are different ways of calming down that can be learned. Your job is to try out these different tools and find the ones that work for you. This first cool-down tool, "A Safe Place," asks you to use your imagination.

At bedtime, Jenna often thought about all the difficult things that happened to her during the day. That made it really hard for her to fall asleep. She would actually become more and more awake as she thought about these unpleasant things. Jenna learned to imagine a safe place. She thought about a perfect place where everything would go well for her. Doing that helped Jenna to relax, not think about her day, and fall asleep.

directions

Draw a picture of your favorite safe place. It can be a place that you have been to, a place you'd like to go to, or a place from your imagination. Give the place a name.

As you look at your picture, try to imagine what it would be like to really be there. What would it smell like? What would the air feel like?

_____

_____

_____

When something is upsetting you, you can always visit this place in your imagination. That can be a good way to calm down.

take note

Different cool-down tools work for different people. It's important for you to figure out which ones work for you so that you can use them.

Were you able to imagine a safe place?

☐ Yes ☐ No

If yes, describe a time when you used your safe place.

_____

_____

_____

_____

_____

_____

_____

_____

_____

_____

Did it help?

☐ Yes ☐ No

If no, try a different cool-down tool. The following activities give you more tools to try.

18 cool-down tools: deep breaths

you need to know

Slow, deep breathing is an automatic way to calm down. When most people become upset, their breathing becomes fast and shallow. Changing your breathing is a great way to cool down anywhere, anytime.

Connor thought of himself as a good math student. Before tests, he studied for hours so that he could feel confident about doing well. Being prepared was important to Connor. Whenever the teacher gave a surprise quiz, Connor panicked. His breathing became shallow and rapid, his palms became sweaty, and he couldn't recall any of the math he usually knew. Connor remembered learning how to take slow, deep breaths to calm himself. He did that for a minute or two and was able to take the test and do very well.

directions

Slow, deep breathing can help you calm down when you are upset. Try the following:

> Lie down on the floor or on your bed and put a book on your abdomen. As you breathe in through your nose, the book should gently rise up. As you breathe out through your mouth, your abdomen should flatten out, and you will see the book go down.

Breathe very slowly or you'll get dizzy. Repeat five times to see how calm you can feel! Once you are comfortable using this technique, it might be fun to teach other people in your family.

Note: Doing this breathing exercise along with picturing your safe place may help you calm down even more.

take note

Were you able to breathe slowly and deeply?

☐ Yes ☐ No

If yes, describe a time when you used breathing to calm yourself.

_____

_____

_____

_____

Did it help?

☐ Yes ☐ No

If no, ask someone for help. Learning how to do this can be harder than it seems!

List places where you think you can use this cool-down tool.

_____

_____

_____

_____

Note: The more you practice this cool-down tool, the more your body will do it all by itself, without your even thinking about it!

you need to know

When they are having difficult feelings, some people keep them a secret. They think that if they ignore these feelings, they will go away. What usually happens, however, is that the feelings get bigger and bigger and become more upsetting over time. Although telling someone about how you feel is always a great idea, sometimes it's not possible. At those times, drawing a picture or writing about how you feel can be a great cool-down tool.

Sean loved to play video games. He often played with his little brother, who was not as good at playing them. When his brother seemed to be ignoring advice that would make him a better player, Sean sometimes got frustrated, which often led to a fight. Sean's counselor gave him a journal and asked him to draw his feelings. Sean found that if he drew his feelings of frustration about his brother, he would be calmer the next time he had to deal with him while playing video games. If Sean wanted to, he could share these drawings with his counselor or he could keep them private.

It's helpful to have a sketchbook or journal that you can easily find so that when something is upsetting you, you can draw a picture or write about what's happening to make you feel the way you do. You might be surprised at how helpful it can be!

directions

In the space below, draw or write about something that happened to make you angry today. Practicing this cool-down tool can help you see if it works for you.

take note

Did your feelings change as a result of drawing or writing?

☐ Yes ☐ No

If yes, describe how your feelings changed.

_____

_____

_____

If no, try a different cool-down tool.

List places where you think you can use this cool-down tool.

_____

_____

_____

List places where you think you can't use this cool-down tool. For example, some teachers will let you draw during class and some won't. If you are not allowed to use this tool at school, try a different one.

_____

_____

_____

Do you feel comfortable sharing these drawings with anyone? If so, with whom?

_____

20 cool-down tools: things that make me happy

Kareem was having a bad day. He got to school late and had to go to the office before class, which made him even later. He was having a test during first period and was very stressed because he had less time to take the test. He went from the test to gym class and realized that he had forgotten to put his gym clothes in his backpack. He got detention for not being prepared. While Kareem was sitting in detention he couldn't stop thinking about all these upsetting events. He realized he was making his hands into fists and mumbling angrily to himself. He remembered a time he spent with his counselor, who helped him focus on cooling down when he got this angry by thinking positive thoughts about what he liked and looked forward to. At that time, Kareem had made a collage that included pictures of his dog. He was able to focus on the idea of spending time with his dog later that day.

While you are upset, changing what you are thinking about can sometimes help calm you. Looking at or thinking about pictures of things that make you happy can help you switch your negative thoughts to more positive ones.

directions

Looking at your "Things That Make Me Happy" creation, list some of the things that make you happy.

_____

_____

_____

_____

_____

_____

_____

_____

_____

_____

_____

_____

_____

_____

_____

_____

_____

take note

Thinking about happy things can change your negative feelings to positive ones. Did this happen when you looked at your creation and made the list? If it did, you can memorize what you wrote, drew, or collaged so that you can recall it when you're upset and don't have the creation with you.

If looking at your creation did not change your negative feelings to positive ones, use a different cool-down tool.

go with the flow 21

you need to know

One of the ways people stay happy, calm, and able to make and keep friends is to become flexible in their thinking. For some of us, being flexible is difficult. We have pictures in our minds of how things should go and we can't let go of those pictures. People like that are sometimes referred to as being rigid or inflexible.

Kerry was asked to join three other girls to go to the movies on Saturday. She was really excited and spent the whole week thinking about what she would wear, what the movie would be like, and what snacks everyone would buy. When Saturday came and the four girls met at Sandy's house, two of the girls said they weren't in the mood to see the movie and wanted to go bowling instead. Sandy said that would be okay with her. Kerry, who didn't like to bowl all that much, was so disappointed and frustrated about this change of plan that she protested in a loud, whiny voice. The other girls asked Kerry what the big deal was. They couldn't understand her attitude. Kerry, who couldn't be flexible enough to go along with the change of plan, refused to go bowling and insisted that they all go to the movies. The three girls didn't agree, so they went bowling and Kerry went home.

If Kerry were more flexible, she could have told herself that she was disappointed but that "majority rules." She could have let go of her expectation and realized that things change sometimes and that being with her friends was the most important part of the day's plan. She could then have decided to stay with her friends and go bowling.

Kerry's inability to go with the flow left her friends annoyed with her. They saw her behavior as another example of her always wanting things her way. They began to feel that it wasn't worth asking Kerry to do things with them anymore.

It would have been easy for Kerry to walk away from this experience thinking her friends were at fault, which would have prevented her from learning how friendships can work more successfully. When Kerry went home and told her mom what happened, she thought her mom would side with her and blame her friends for being unfair. Kerry's mom was able to calmly and kindly tell Kerry that her choice was a good example of her tendency to be rigid when dealing with other people. Kerry and her mom agreed to talk about it whenever Mom noticed Kerry being rigid in her relationships.

directions

Knowing how to handle an unexpected change can help you become more flexible and go with the flow. Parents, counselors, therapists, or people who understand you really well can give you valuable feedback that lets you know when your inflexible thinking gets in your way.

Whom do you think you could trust to help you learn to see this part of yourself more clearly?

_____

Ask these people to help you learn more about your tendency to be inflexible. Let them know that you need feedback so that you can learn to catch yourself when you begin to take a rigid stance. Some people like to use a code word or gesture so that the person giving the feedback can signal you discreetly.

Once you have asked for this type of feedback, keep notes here describing your experience and what type of situations you tend to be inflexible in. Notice any patterns. For example, ask yourself these questions:

- Are you flexible about things at home and inflexible at school?
- Are you flexible at school and inflexible at home?
- Are you flexible or inflexible with certain people? Whom?
- What happens when plans change?
- What happens when you are tired or hungry?
- What happens when unexpected things happen?
- What happens when you don't get your way?
- What happens when you disagree about rules?
- What happens when you need to stop doing something you like doing?

_____

_____

_____

_____

take note

Once the person helping you gives you feedback, rate on the scale below how much you agree or disagree with that feedback.

1	2	3	4	5
Totally agree		Somewhat agree		Totally disagree

If you picked a 4 or 5 on this scale, it may be helpful to ask other people you trust to review this information with you. If they see your behavior in the same way the first person did, it may be that they have a clearer sense of when you become inflexible than you do. That is not unusual, as it is often difficult for people to see how something that is so automatic and natural to them could be something others see as a problem.

Once you become more aware of the types of situations that cause you to become inflexible, do you think you can catch yourself so that you need less feedback from others and can rely on tuning in to yourself for this information?

Once you are able to catch yourself, is it easy or difficult for you to find strategies to let go of your rigidity (for example, cool-down tools, the image of changing the plan in your head, etc.) and go with the flow?

_____

_____

It is a good idea to come up with another visual icon that can help you remember how to do this.

22 be prepared

you need to know

Some people have a hard time when they think something is going to happen in a certain way and then it doesn't go that way. It is as if they had pictures in their heads and really want those pictures to become what happens. One way to avoid this type of unsettling experience is to prepare yourself when you are going into a new situation or a situation that has the potential to develop in a variety of ways. When you consider all the different ways a situation may turn out, you prepare yourself for the unexpected.

Allie had always wanted to go to a school dance but was intimidated by the prospect of a gym full of students. Her counselor and her mom were encouraging her to go to the upcoming dance. Knowing that Allie would be nervous, her counselor suggested that she prepare for the event. She had Allie ask other girls to describe what dances were like. Next, Allie sat down with her counselor and wrote a list of details that were included in all the descriptions. From this list, Allie knew that there would probably be decorations in the gym, food and drinks available, music (possibly louder than she liked), and kids hanging around in groups and dancing while chaperones looked on. She also learned that it was okay for a group of girls to dance together. Allie's anxiety was lowered when she heard that because she thought she would only get to dance if a boy asked her. Even though Allie was convinced that no one would ask, her counselor had her rehearse what she would do if a boy came up and asked her to dance, which might just happen! Allie practiced how she might respond to different boys she knew, while the counselor pretended to be those boys. They also brushed up on Allie's conversation skills, especially those skills needed to enter into a conversation with a group, as she was almost certain she would need to seek out a group to hang out with.

At the dance, Allie found many of the details from her list were correct. The music was louder than she liked, but since she had prepared herself, it did not bother her as much as it normally did. Looking around, Allie saw decorations, food and drinks, and groups of kids. She spotted some girls she knew from English class and and joined their conversation. A boy she knew from Science class asked her to dance, and even though he wasn't one of the boys she had thought about when she was rehearsing with her counselor, she knew what to say and danced with him. When Allie got home, she thought about the evening. She had done it! Her fear had been that she wouldn't know what to do at the dance. However, she was prepared, and while she wasn't completely comfortable, she managed to have a good time. Allie was surprised at her success and eager to tell her counselor that their preparations for this event had helped!

directions

For this activity, ask an adult you trust to work with you.

1. Think about an upcoming event that will put you in a situation you haven't been in before—a wedding, your first dance, an overnight school trip—where you don't know what to expect.

2. With the adult, fill in the sections below. Make sure you consider lots of possibilities.

    Name of event: _____

    Facts I know about the event (time, place, sounds, sights, lights): _____

    _____

    _____

    _____

    Things that will probably happen at the event (people you may see, what you may do, what might happen): _____

    _____

    _____

Things that you think won't happen, but could possibly happen (like Allie's being asked to dance): _____

_____

_____

3. Look at the facts you listed. Is there anything listed that makes you feel uncomfortable?

    _____

    _____

    _____

4. If so, come up with ways to cope with these difficulties.

    _____

    _____

    _____

5. Next, look at the things you think will probably happen at this event. Are your expectations realistic? If not, list some other probabilities and how you would cope with any that might make you feel uncomfortable. Here is where your trusted adult helper comes in handy!

    _____

    _____

    _____

6. Next, look at the things you think won't happen at this event, but may. List ways to prepare yourself for these possibilities.

    _____

    _____

    _____

take note

After you've attended the event you prepared for, it's a good idea to review what actually happened and compare it to what you thought would happen. See how good you were at predicting what would happen and how good you were about preparing for it.

If you had difficulty with this activity, make sure you ask for help the next time you attempt to prepare for another event. It can take time and practice to develop this skill so that you can do it on your own.

23 gathering and processing social information

you need to know

The social world can be a confusing place for people who do not automatically pick up social cues. As kids get older and become teens, this world becomes more complicated and subtle. In any given social situation, being aware of people's reactions and feelings can make picking up social cues a bit easier. Once you observe lots of situations, you can get better at predicting how someone will react or feel. That makes it easier to get along with people.

One day at lunch, Sam noticed that Daniel was quieter than usual. Sam remembered that on most days Daniel made jokes and laughed while he ate. He asked Daniel if something was wrong. Daniel told Sam that he had gotten a bad grade on his biology test, and he was surprised and upset because he had thought he had done well on it. Sam hadn't realized that Daniel was concerned about his grades. He always seemed so cheerful all the time at school. Sam learned something new about Daniel by paying attention to him.

directions

Gather social information from the people around you. It's important to do this in a way that other people will not notice. It's best to start with your family because it is okay to check with people afterward to see if your guesses about their feelings and actions were accurate. Also your family probably won't mind if you make mistakes. You may learn the most by recording social interactions that confused you or involved someone reacting in a very different way than you thought they would. Asking them for feedback later will be an important part of gathering this information.

Look over the following questions; you can answer them with information about anyone you observe. Use the space below the questions to write your answers. Here's an example to help you get started:

> Notice something that makes someone in your family happy. What was it? How did you know the person was happy? What did his or her face and body look like? After you've written your answers, ask if the person was feeling happy, and why.

Pam was watching her mom. She wrote:

> My mom was happy when she got a phone call. I could tell she was happy because she smiled and laughed while talking. She sat in a chair and looked comfortable. When I asked her later if she had been happy, she said she was happy because her sister called with good news.

Observation 1: Notice something that makes someone in your family happy. What was it? How did you know the person was happy? What did his or her face and body look like?

_____

_____

_____

_____

Ask if the person was feeling happy, and why. If you guessed correctly, go on to the next question. If you had difficulty identifying what the person was feeling or reacting to, write down where your perception and the other person's reality did not match.

_____

_____

Observation 2: Notice something that makes someone in your family angry. What was it? How did you know the person was angry? What did his or her face and body look like?

_____

_____

_____

_____

Ask if the person was feeling angry, and why. If you guessed correctly, go on to the next question. If you had difficulty identifying what the person was feeling or reacting to, write down where your perception and the other person's reality did not match.

_____

_____

Observation 3: Notice something that makes someone in your family sad. What was it? How did you know the person was sad? What did his or her face and body look like?

_____

_____

_____

_____

Ask if the person was feeling sad, and why. If you guessed correctly, go on to the next question. If you had difficulty identifying what the person was feeling or reacting to, write down where your perception and the other person's reality did not match.

_____

_____

Observation 4: Notice something that makes someone in your family surprised. What was it? How did you know the person was surprised? What did his or her face and body look like?

_____

_____

_____

_____

Ask if the person was feeling surprised, and why. If you had difficulty identifying what the person was feeling or reacting to, write down where your perception and the other person's reality did not match.

_____

_____

take note

Now that you've done this activity, you are on your way to developing the skill to gather and process social information. Since you've already practiced at home, now try to make guesses about what other people are feeling at school and in other places in your life. You may want to practice in the following situations:

- In a store

- In the library

- At a family party or gathering

- At a vacation spot

- In a restaurant

Practice gathering information about how people interact. Make guesses about what's behind people's behaviors and how they might be feeling. This exercise is for you to get better at noticing things, so it's a good idea to keep these observations to yourself. If you are with someone you trust, you can run your guesses by them to see if they agree with you. Talk about how you both came to your conclusions.

This exercise will also help you pay closer attention to what's going on around you, which is an important step to making better social connections and avoiding negative social interactions.

Krista is in history class when the teacher tells the students to break into groups of four to work on a research project. Krista assumes that she will be asked to join a group with Rodrigo, Sean, and Tiffany because she had worked with them on the last project for this class. When she turns in their direction, she sees that they have already found a fourth partner. Krista automatically thinks, "They must hate me….What did I do wrong?…I'm always left out….I have no friends…." As these thoughts run through her head, she feels sad and hopeless and she can't focus on finding a different group to partner with.

What would help Krista in the future would be to develop the ability to counter her negative self-talk with positive statements. That entails being aware of her negative self-talk and accepting that what she tells herself might not be the truth, for example, "Rodrigo, Sean, and Tiffany don't hate me or think I've done anything wrong; they just included a girl who had walked up to them and asked if she could join them."

directions

Becoming aware of your negative self-talk is the first step toward changing it. Filling in the following chart can help you keep track of what you tell yourself, how often you engage in negative self-talk, and in what circumstances.

Date	Time	Where Are You? What Are You Doing?	Negative Self-Talk
11/17	7 AM	At home, looking for homework	I'm such a loser.
11/17	12 PM	In the lunchroom, looking for a seat	No one likes me.

take note

Were you surprised about the frequency of your negative self-talk?

☐ Yes ☐ No

If you notice any patterns in the times, places, or situations that trigger your negative self-talk, describe them here. Recognizing these patterns will help you become more aware of when negative self-talk is a problem for you.

_____

_____

_____

_____

_____

_____

_____

_____

_____

_____

_____

_____

_____

_____

_____

_____

25 creating new self-talk

you need to know

With practice and awareness, you can counteract your negative self-talk by creating positive statements to replace your negative thoughts. Many people believe that their negative self-talk contains the truth, but in reality it is often based on misperceptions, exaggerations, and mistaken beliefs. Changing your negative self-talk can decrease your anxiety and change your attitude so that you can have a better chance of feeling good about yourself. When people feel good about themselves, others feel comfortable being with them.

In activity 24, Krista experienced negative self-talk when she felt excluded from the group she wanted to join. The story below shows how Krista worked to develop positive counter-thoughts.

Krista is in history class when the teacher tells the students to break into groups of four to work on a research project. Krista assumes that she will be asked to join a group with Rodrigo, Sean, and Tiffany because she had worked with them on the last project for this class. When she turns in their direction, she sees that they have already found a fourth partner. Krista automatically thinks, "They must hate me....What did I do wrong?...I'm always left out....I have no friends...." As these thoughts run through her head, Krista realizes that she is engaging in negative self-talk. After class, Krista uses the chart her counselor gave her and records the information about her negative self-talk. She later takes it to her counselor, and they work on developing positive counter-thoughts. Here is what they came up with.

Negative Self-Talk	Positive Counter-Thought
They must hate me.	Just because they chose someone else doesn't mean they hate me.
What did I do wrong?	Just because things don't go as I expect them to go doesn't mean I did anything wrong.
I'm always left out.	I can change my situation.
I have no friends.	I am learning to take risks in making friends

directions

Developing positive counter-thoughts is the next step in changing your negative self-talk. List the negative self-talk you wrote in activity 24 and then list positive counter-thoughts. Developing positive counter-thoughts can be a difficult task. If you have a hard time doing it on your own, ask someone you trust for help. Below is a list of examples to help you start your own chart.

Negative Self-Talk	Positive Counter-Thought
I'm such a loser.	I like myself and accept myself the way I am.
I'm so stupid.	It's okay if I don't always have an answer.

take note

How hard or easy was it for you to create positive counter-thoughts?

_____

_____

_____

The difficulty in coming up with positive counter-thoughts can come from a number of things:

- Messages you were given as a child from family or other people in your life

- Believing that only outside circumstances determine how you feel about yourself, instead of believing that how you deal with those circumstances can determine how you feel

- Believing in a negative world view and being so used to thinking in a negative way

- Low self-esteem

- A problem in deciding which positive statements fit which negative thoughts

If you can identify one or more of the above as what made this assignment difficult for you, ask someone you trust for help. Turning negative self-talk around can be difficult, so someone who seems to think in a positive way is a good person to ask.

using positive self-talk

you need to know

With practice and awareness, you can counteract your negative self-talk by creating positive statements to replace those negative thoughts. Now that you have gotten used to counteracting negative thoughts, it's time to practice!

In activity 25, Krista worked with her counselor on developing positive counter-thoughts for her negative self-talk. Once she got the hang of it, it was time for her to put it into action. Krista practiced by using the chart you will see later in this activity. The story below shows how Krista changed her negative thinking and how that changed what happened next.

Krista is in history class when the teacher tells the students to break into groups of four to work on a research project. Krista assumes that she will be asked to join a group with Rodrigo, Sean, and Tiffany because she had worked with them on the last project for this class. When she turns in their direction, she sees that they have already found a fourth partner. Krista automatically thinks, "I'm such a loser." She realizes that she is engaging in negative self-talk and stops herself. She takes a deep breath and remembers the positive counter-thought that she had worked on with her counselor. She tells herself, "I like myself and accept myself the way I am." Krista is then able to move on and focus on the situation at hand. Looking around the room, she finds a group of three students and walks over to ask if she can join them.

directions

Choose a day to try this out. When you wake up that day, tell yourself that you are going to counter one negative thought with a positive counter-thought. You will need to be aware of your negative self-talk, and, in the moment, come up with a positive counter-thought. Record below what this was like for you.

Date	Time	Where Are You? What Are You Doing?	Negative Self-Talk	Positive Counter-Thoughts

take note

Did changing your negative self-talk change your feeling or mood at the time? How?

_____

_____

This technique generally takes a lot of repetition to work. It may feel unnatural at first, but it is a big job to change something that has become a habit over a long period of time. Keep at it!

Once this technique works for you, you will want to use it more often. The chart below is like the one you used earlier to record your successes. You may want to copy it and have it handy in your pocket or backpack.

Date	Time	Where Are You? What Are You Doing?	Negative Self-Talk	Positive Counter-Thoughts

27 rules

you need to know

There are all kinds of rules in our society: rules that are laws, game rules, rules of social behavior, family rules, and school rules, to name a few. Some, like legal rules and game rules, are written. Other rules are discussed, may be unwritten, and are assumed to be commonly understood by the members of a group (family group, school, friendships). People have all kinds of feelings and reactions to rules. Some people are very strict about following and enforcing rules, while others are more relaxed about them.

Sometimes, people who have difficulty with social skills have a tendency to rely heavily on rules, feeling that life without rules would be chaos. When rule-dependent people encounter situations when they feel others are not following the rules, they become anxious. Often that leads to conflict with people who may not be as dependent on the rules to give them a sense of security.

Brianna was a rule-dependent person. She always made sure she knew all the school rules and prided herself on always following them. One day at school, she encountered a group of girls in her grade who were breaking a school rule by hanging posters on the hallway walls. Brianna told the girls to stop because seeing the posters on the wall made her anxious. Brianna was accustomed to poster-free hallways. She was unaware that the girls had been given permission to hang posters because it was Spirit Week at school. The girls laughed at Brianna and told her to mind her own business. People passing by weren't bothered by the posters. Some of them even complimented the girls who were hanging them up.

directions

Think about what rules mean to you. Circle the number that shows how you think you would feel in the following situations:

You see someone break the law (for example, someone driving above the speed limit).

1	2	3	4	5	6	7	8	9	10
Calm				Agitated				Extremely anxious and/or angry	

You are playing a game and someone mentions a rule you do not know about, and you can't check the rule book.

1	2	3	4	5	6	7	8	9	10
Calm				Agitated				Extremely anxious and/or angry	

You think someone is breaking the rule or cheating.

1	2	3	4	5	6	7	8	9	10
Calm				Agitated				Extremely anxious and/or angry	

You hear someone cursing.

1	2	3	4	5	6	7	8	9	10
Calm				Agitated				Extremely anxious and/or angry	

You see someone smoking at school.

1	2	3	4	5	6	7	8	9	10
Calm				Agitated				Extremely anxious and/or angry	

You see someone cutting class at school.

1	2	3	4	5	6	7	8	9	10
Calm				Agitated				Extremely anxious and/or angry	

take note

If you scored on the high end in this activity, the following self-talk might be helpful when you are in a situation where your anxiety or anger about broken rules will result in a confrontation that has a high social cost.

- Things are not going the way I thought they would. I will be okay.

- It's only a game. I am choosing friendship over adherence to game rules.

- Even though someone is breaking a rule, it doesn't have anything to do directly with me, and no one is in danger.

- Rules sometimes change in different settings. I need time to think about this setting and situation. I will be okay.

- Sometimes there are unspoken rules that I don't understand. I can ask for help.

- Even though rules are being broken, my world won't fall apart. I will be okay.

- I can go with the flow!

You can also use some of the cool-down tools you learned earlier in this book. A few deep breaths can go a long way when you are about to quickly react to someone else's behavior.

you need to know

The social world we live in has many unwritten rules of behavior. Some people seem to just know these rules. Their brains help them intuit things about the social world without much trouble. Other people need to learn these rules. They need social rules pointed out to them in order to get the hang of social situations. Often, they have a difficult time understanding the necessity of these rules, and sometimes they even reject the idea of having to learn about them. Unfortunately, thinking this way makes it difficult to live and work in our society. While it may never make sense to you to follow some of these rules, you need to know how important they are in terms of how others may see and respond to you. Important life skills, such as finding and keeping a job, making and keeping friends and acquaintances, and living with other people, rely on everyone following many of these rules to some extent.

Charlie came to see his counselor, Beth, every week. As Charlie entered her office, Beth would greet him with a smile and say, "Hi there, Charlie. How are you today?" Charlie, not looking directly at Beth, would mumble an answer and sit down. One day Beth asked Charlie why he never asked her how she was. Charlie told Beth that he really didn't care how she was that day—no offense! Beth, knowing that Charlie was seeing her because of his difficulty with social situations, explained to Charlie that many times when people ask, "How are you?" they really don't care how you are, but that asking is a socially accepted way of greeting someone. Charlie was confused. Why do people ask if they don't care? Isn't that being dishonest? Beth explained that some social rules may not fit Charlie's preference for only doing what he sees fit, but living this way will leave Charlie at a big disadvantage—people will not accept him or his ideas if he cannot engage in the minimum of what is considered polite and socially acceptable.

How people resolve this conflict has a great impact on how they succeed in the world. Those who accept that they have to live by the world's rules and go through the process of learning and practicing social rules can often get more satisfaction from their relationships with others. They can work on getting what they want out of life, such as a college education, a satisfying job, a family of their own, and friends. Those who cannot accept that they have to live by these rules often spend a lot of time and energy trying to get others to live by their rules. They usually end up in conflict-laden, disappointing relationships or are unable to even form relationships.

There are many other unwritten rules of social behavior in addition to asking, "How are you?" Some of these rules involve conversation, and some involve body language, as in the following examples:

- When you are speaking to other people, it is expected that you will make eye contact with them.

- When people ask you how your vacation was, it is expected that you will answer and then ask whether they took vacations and if they enjoyed them.

- When people are walking close behind you and you open a door, it is expected that you will hold the door open for them.

- When people ask you about your interests, it is expected that you will ask them if they are interested in similar things, and if not, what they are interested in.

Some of these rules depend on the country you are in. In the United States, these are common social rules:

- When you first meet someone who extends a hand to you, it is expected that you will shake that person's hand.

- When you first meet someone who asks you a question, it is expected that you will look at that person and reply within a matter of a few seconds.

directions

Wherever you go for the next few days, observe people: family members, people at school, people in stores, people in restaurants, and so on. As in activity 23, try not to draw attention to yourself.

What behaviors do you see that seem strange or unnecessary to you? Keep a journal with you so that you can write down some of these behaviors.

List five of them here:

1. _____

2. _____

3. _____

4. _____

5. _____

Why did you think each behavior was strange or unnecessary? Can you understand why people acted the way they did?

_____

_____

_____

_____

_____

_____

_____

_____

take note

With someone you trust, discuss your observations and how you analyzed what you noticed. Have that person explain to you why the social rules you noticed exist and what they mean to other people. Consider, for example, "When you ask me how I am, I feel cared about by you, even if you don't actually care. That helps me to be friendlier to you. If you say 'Good morning. How are you?' when you get to your job each day, people smile and appreciate your concern and politeness."

Which of the examples you listed can you see yourself becoming comfortable doing?

_____

_____

_____

_____

_____

_____

Which ones would be too difficult or uncomfortable for you to do? Why?

_____

_____

_____

_____

_____

_____

Your behavior with other people either increases or decreases your chances of making friends.

Most people like there to be a give-and-take of ideas and opinions in friendships. People who have difficulty with social skills often are convinced that being right is more important than considering the other person's point of view. They choose being right over being friends. Acting like the "rule police"—being controlling, bossy, or rigid with other people—can make it difficult for them to want to be friends with you. Even when you think you are right, it is important to listen to the other person's side of a situation. Conversation can then grow out of both points of view.

The price you might pay when you insist on being controlling, bossy, rigid, or always right is a kind of social cost. If you can begin thinking about what the social cost might be as a result of different ways you behave, you can make more sense out of the way people react to you.

directions

Below are some friendship equations that add behaviors together to show the social cost of behaving in certain ways.

Being bossy about rules or doing things your way
+ Not listening to how someone else wants to do things
———————————————————————————————————————
= The other person becoming annoyed and not wanting to be around you

Calmly discussing the rules
+ Compromising about the rules
———————————————————————————————————————
= Your friend wanting to be with you

Having a negative opinion about something your friend likes a lot
+ Insisting on imposing that negative opinion on your friend
———————————————————————————————————————
= Your friend not wanting to be with you

Insisting on doing only what you are interested in
+ Not thinking about what your friend wants to do
———————————————————————————————————————
= (Fill in the answer.)

Playing games that your friends want to play that aren't your favorite
+ Showing interest and playing to the end of the game
———————————————————————————————————————
= (Fill in the answer.)

Checking the rules a lot during the game
+ Not listening to what your friends say about the rules
———————————————————————————————————————
= (Fill in the answer.)

take note

List five things you do that help your chances of connecting with other people.

1. _____

2. _____

3. _____

4. _____

5. _____

List five things you do that may cause other people to avoid getting to know you better.

1. _____

2. _____

3. _____

4. _____

5. _____

Ask your parents or adults you trust to think about what they see you do when you are with other people. Can they list some things you already do that help you connect?

_____

_____

_____

Ask your parents or adults you trust to think about what they see you do when you are with other people. Can they list some things you do that may cause people to avoid being with you?

_____

_____

_____

30 being aware

you need to know

Being aware of what is going on around you is an important skill to learn. It will help you find opportunities to connect with others and ways to be aware of, and avoid, negative social interactions. People with social-skills difficulties sometimes tend to daydream or escape into fantasies when they get overwhelmed, leaving them unaware of what is going on around them.

In every school, some kids are bullies, some are victims, and some are innocent bystanders. And from school to school, the percentages don't change! What do you think these percentages are? In a school of one hundred children, how many do you think are bullies? How many are victims? How many stand by and watch?

Actually, in a group of one hundred, nine children would be bullies, eleven would be victims, and eighty would stand by and watch. These numbers surprise many people.

What do you think the eighty kids do to avoid being picked on? Most of them are kids who are not often alone. They also are very aware of what is going on around them and who is near them, and they are good at guessing what other people are thinking and feeling. That helps them avoid people who can be mean.

How do they know how to do it? Some people have a natural talent. They are always tuned in to everything going on around them. Other people like to daydream. Their thoughts go to places in their imaginations or to topics they have an intense interest in. While it may feel good to be focused on these other things in your head, especially when the real events in front of you may be overwhelming, daydreaming makes it hard to notice the world around you.

directions

Read the following stories:

Jeffrey went to the local bookstore to see the newest video game magazines. As he was absorbed in reading one, a group of kids walked by and tried to see what Jeffrey was reading. Jeffrey was so absorbed in his magazine that he didn't even notice these kids. They surrounded Jeffrey and began bumping into him and harassing him. Caught off guard, Jeffrey tried to walk away. The kids prevented him from doing so. Jeffrey became frightened and began to panic, making the kids laugh and harass him even more. Finally a store clerk helped Jeffrey by asking the kids to leave the store.

Do you think Jeffrey could have done anything differently? ☐ Yes ☐ No

If yes, how could he have avoided being harassed by those kids?

_____

_____

_____

Maria was sitting alone in her school cafeteria. Two girls came over to her table and sat down. They began discussing a film they had watched in class that day. Maria had also seen this film, but she didn't join in the conversation; instead, she was thinking about a TV show she was looking forward to later that evening. When Maria went to see her counselor, she expressed her sadness about not having friends.

Do you think Maria could have done anything differently? ☐ Yes ☐ No

If yes, what?

_____

_____

_____

take note

We want you to practice staying aware and paying attention to things that are going on around you. For example, when you are with your family at dinner, notice the following:

What is each person talking about? _____

_____

_____

What is each person doing? _____

_____

_____

List three other things you notice about each person:

1. _____

2. _____

3. _____

1. _____

2. _____

3. _____

1. _____

2. _____

3. _____

We hope that you can practice with your family so that noticing what's going on around you when you are with peers becomes easier.

conversation skills 31

you need to know

Part of connecting with others is knowing how to engage in a meaningful conversation with them. Being with others is an important way to help you to stay safe, because kids who are picked on are often alone.

Whether you are talking to one person or to a group of people, it may help you to think of a conversation as a tennis match. One person speaks (hits the ball) to another person who answers (hits the ball back), and the conversation (tennis game) goes back and forth. If tennis players are not watching (listening) and lose track of the ball (don't pay attention to what the other person is saying), they miss the ball and lose a point.

There are different ways to have a conversation.

Reciprocal Conversation

In this type of conversation, both people listen. They take turns asking questions and show interest by looking at each other.

Talking for Yourself

This type of talk takes place when there are two people speaking but only one person is talking a lot. The person who is talking is not showing much interest in the other person and isn't looking at the person or noticing if that person is bored or interested. If you do talk for yourself a lot, it's important for you to know that, for some people, not finishing their full thought is very difficult. They almost feel like they are driven to finish speaking. Continuing to talk for yourself, however, pushes people away and has a high social cost.

Talking to Yourself

In this type of talk, you say something to yourself, either silently in your head or out loud. If you are saying it out loud, it is best if you are by yourself. Other people might think it is strange and confusing to hear you talk out loud to yourself when you are around them.

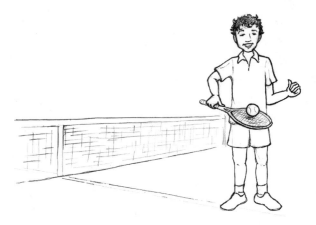

directions

For this activity it will be necessary for you to observe and evaluate yourself in different interactions. On the scale below, rate yourself on how often you do the following:

You have a reciprocal conversation with family members.

1	2	3	4	5	6	7	8	9	10
Never				Sometimes					Always

You have a reciprocal conversation with peers.

1	2	3	4	5	6	7	8	9	10
Never				Sometimes					Always

You talk for yourself with family members.

1	2	3	4	5	6	7	8	9	10
Never				Sometimes					Always

You talk for yourself with peers.

1	2	3	4	5	6	7	8	9	10
Never				Sometimes					Always

You talk to yourself when you are with family members.

1	2	3	4	5	6	7	8	9	10
Never				Sometimes					Always

You talk to yourself when you are with peers.

1	2	3	4	5	6	7	8	9	10
Never				Sometimes					Always

take note

If you rated yourself from 1 to 5 on the "reciprocal conversation" scale, be aware that some people have a difficult time entering into a conversation and knowing how to get into its back-and-forth rhythm. Observing people having conversations is a good way to start understanding how to do it. Practicing with family members or people you trust can be the next step. Having an awareness that this is an area where you need to strengthen your skills will help motivate you to make some changes.

If you rated yourself from 6 to 10 on the "reciprocal conversation" scale, be aware that some people have a difficult time evaluating their own conversation skills. You may want to run your self-assessment by a family member or people you trust to make sure others see your skill level as you do. They may be able to point out areas where they think you could use improvement.

If you rated yourself from 6 to 10 on the "talk for yourself" scale, be aware that for some people, it is very difficult to stop talking about a subject that is stuck in their heads. They feel a real need to finish what they are saying, but they often go on for so long that the other person is left out of the conversation. If you find it difficult to stop talking, you may want to do the following:

- Try to finish the thought silently in your head.

- Write it down.

- Know that you can talk about it later, possibly with someone else.

If you rated yourself from 6 to 10 on the "talk to yourself" scale, be aware that some people find it difficult to stop talking to themselves—either out loud or in their heads—about a topic of great interest to them, even when they are with other people. They are left vulnerable because they are not aware of what is going on around them, and, if they are talking out loud, other people do not understand why they are talking to themselves. You may want to try the techniques in the bulleted list above for stopping these thoughts when you are with other people. You should also know that people who struggle with talking to themselves often resort to doing it when they are overwhelmed or uncomfortable in a situation. Strengthening your social skills will work to decrease this anxiety, and you might not need to focus so much on thoughts that may be comforting to you in times of stress. Talking to yourself is okay to do while you are alone.

you need to know

Have you ever seen a filter? Filters are used in coffee makers, air conditioners, dryers, water purifiers, and so on. The filters in these machines are there to help block out unwanted materials.

Some people need to develop an internal filter system to avoid saying or doing things that might insult people, hurt their feelings, or make them angry. People who can successfully use this type of filter system find it easier to make and keep friends, and they soon realize that people no longer avoid them.

Alex notices that people react to some things he says by arguing, rolling their eyes, laughing, or walking away. That confuses Alex because he doesn't think he is saying anything wrong. Actually, Alex prides himself on always speaking the truth. So what is going wrong?

Alex hasn't yet developed an internal filter system. He believes that speaking his thoughts is a form of honesty. Most people, however, don't say everything they think. They filter their thoughts and keep some of their ideas and opinions to themselves. Here's an example:

> Joy went over to two girls from her biology class. She asked if they were going to study for the test the next day. Tara said she couldn't concentrate on anything because she was upset about her acne. She had a party to go to in a few days and thought her skin looked terrible. Angela said, "Oh, Tara, you look okay. Don't worry." Joy, wanting to give her opinion, said, "Yeah, I've been noticing how you have so many pimples lately!" As tears formed in Tara's eyes, Tara and Angela walked away, horrified. Joy was confused. She had only told the truth. What was wrong with that? Angela, obviously, was lying because Tara's face really did look terrible.

Why would Tara like Angela's response (a lie) better than Joy's (the truth)? When people bring up their own flaws, they are usually looking for reassurance. If Joy had developed a filter, she could have chosen to say nothing, to echo what Angela said, or to say something so general that no offense would be taken, such as, "I hate acne."

directions

For each situation, write what you might say if you had no filter and if you developed a filter:

Your friend does badly on a test and says to you, "I'm so stupid."

Unfiltered answer: _____

_____

Filtered answer: _____

_____

Your mom comes to your room wearing a dress you don't particularly like. With a big smile on her face, she asks you, "How do I look?"

Unfiltered answer: _____

_____

Filtered answer: _____

_____

A group of kids you are sitting with at lunch are talking about a new video game that you think is awful. They all seem to like the game and are excited about getting and playing it.

Unfiltered comment you might make: _____

_____

Filtered comment you might make: _____

_____

take note

If you were able to come up with filtered answers, try to do that in your everyday conversations with people. It can be hard to do it right away. You may find yourself saying some things that are insulting and noticing people's reactions. Later in the day, take the opportunity to think about what happened and come up with a filtered response. Practicing in this way will help you catch yourself the next time, before you say something unfiltered. Don't be too hard on yourself! Real change takes time, patience, and practice.

If you couldn't come up with filtered answers, you need help learning how. Therapists and counselors are trained to help people who have trouble doing it on their own. If learning this skill is important to you, you will be able to learn it with help.

33 choosing your friends

you need to know

Many people look at the popular people and want to be a part of their group. What's more important than being with the popular group is to find friends who treat you well. These people may be the popular ones, or they may not be. How can you tell who would be a good friend?

Ever since the beginning of the school year, Caitlin wanted to be friends with Joy, Madison, and Cara. They always looked like they were having fun. They were often the center of attention, surrounded by people wanting to be with them. When Caitlin tried to speak with these girls, they ignored her. Through the grapevine, she heard that they thought she was a loser and were trying to avoid her. That upset Caitlin, but she thought she should just try harder to make them her friends. The harder she tried, the colder the girls became. After discussing it with her mom, Caitlin looked around at other girls at school and noticed that Maya and Jackie were interested in art, just like she was. She decided to approach Maya and Jackie to see if she could connect with them. When Caitlin complimented Jackie on the drawing she was working on, Maya and Jackie asked Caitlin about her artwork. They got into a discussion about anime art and became very excited that they all loved that art form. Maya and Jackie asked Caitlin to meet them in the lunchroom the next day.

directions

1.   Make a list of peers you know.

_____   _____

_____   _____

_____   _____

_____   _____

_____   _____

2.   Look below at the list that describes the behavior of friendly and unfriendly peers.

Friendly Behavior

- Greets you when he or she sees you
- Asks you to hang out
- Helps you when you need help
- Shares with you
- Does what you want to do some of the time

Unfriendly Behavior

- Harasses you
- Tries to hurt you physically
- Laughs at you; gets others to laugh at you
- Ignores you
- Bosses you around

3.   Think about how the people you listed behave toward you. Next to each name, put a check for every friendly behavior and an X for every unfriendly behavior shown by that person.

take note

Look back at the list of people you made. Do you see more checks or Xs? If you see mostly checks, you are doing a good job of choosing people to be with. If you see more Xs, you may need to come up with a new plan for finding friends. Here are some suggestions:

- Look around at all the people you have a chance to be with, even ones that you may not have been interested in before.

- Notice their behaviors and look for people who are acting in friendly ways. Keep in mind the list of friendly behaviors on the preceding page.

- Try entering into conversation with these people and notice which ones treat you well.

- Remember, when you choose friends, it's not important how popular they are. What matters is how they treat you.

If you have a hard time finding people you want to be with, ask for help at school. A counselor may be able to point out some friendly peers for you to get to know.

you need to know

There are different levels of friendship. When you know the level of friendship you have with someone, it's easier to know what to expect from them and what they expect from you.

Story 1

Carlos joined the robotics club at school. He knew some of the kids, but some were new to him. Lena was assigned to work on a project with Carlos. Carlos had seen Lena around school but didn't know her. They worked well together, and Carlos thought Lena would want to be good friends outside the club. Carlos began instant messaging Lena on the computer the very night he met her. From his messages, Lena realized that Carlos thought they were best buddies. She was polite but kept her responses very short because when Lena met someone new, it took her a long time to feel comfortable. Her best friends were people she had known for a long time. Carlos didn't have many friends, so when someone was kind to him, he came on very strong. At the next club meeting, Lena teamed up with someone else because she was uncomfortable with Carlos's eagerness to be such close friends. Carlos was surprised and disappointed.

Story 2

Alexa stayed to herself at school. She ate lunch by herself and hung out alone. Alexa was into martial arts and attended the martial arts club at school. Julie, the president of the club, welcomed Alexa and asked her to join the other kids in planning a demonstration for the school on Club Day. Although Alexa stayed to herself and didn't participate in this discussion, in her mind she felt very much a part of the plan. The other kids in the club didn't know why Alexa was there since she wasn't participating, and they ignored her. When Club Day came, Alexa showed up at the demonstration and Julie told her that there wasn't a part for her. Alexa was confused and upset. She thought that she was a part of the club and that Julie was her friend.

When children are young, it's a little easier for them to know and understand different levels of friendship: the one or two friends they are very close with are their best friends, a few kids they know and like and play with sometimes are friends, and lots of kids they just know are acquaintances.

As kids get older and become teens, this idea becomes more complicated. Some people feel comfortable becoming very friendly quickly, and some people don't. For some people, the group they hang around with becomes an important part of their identity. Instead of a best friend, the group becomes the "best friend." For some kids, this group is where they stay and they don't become friends with anyone outside of their clique. Other kids associate themselves with lots of groups, for example, a group of kids they grew up with, a group of kids from a club they attend, and a group of kids they eat lunch with.

directions

To help yourself understand the levels of friends in your life, draw a friendship solar system with yourself as the sun. The ring nearest to you will show your closest friends, the next ring your friends, and the last ring your acquaintances. See the example below to help you.

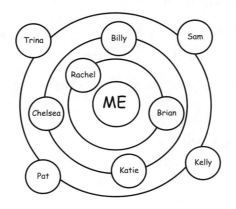

take note

Looking at the friendship solar system you created, notice which ring you placed each person in. With an adult you trust, consider the following:

- How much time do you spend with each of these people?
- How long have you known these people?
- Do you see them outside of school?
- Do they invite you to spend time with them?
- Do you talk about things you are both interested in?
- Do you trust each other?
- Do they help you when you ask?
- Do they cheer you up when you are upset?
- Are they kind to you?

Keeping these questions in mind, write each person's name below and determine how many of the above questions fit each person. They won't all apply to everyone you know. However the purpose of this exercise is to help you have a deeper understanding of where you fit in the social world around you.

Name	Notes

you need to know

Some people are very flexible. They can move from one activity to another very easily, stop a thought in their heads from repeating itself, and talk about many different subjects. Other people become stuck, and they need to learn how to be more flexible. When you are stuck, it's hard for people to be with you.

You know you are stuck when these things happen:

- You have a thought in your head and can't stop thinking about it.

- You want to talk about a certain subject and can't stop talking about it.

- Something unexpected happens, and you need to change your plan, but you can't let go of the old plan.

In all these cases, remaining stuck makes it difficult to be with people or for them to want to be with you. They don't understand why you don't get unstuck, because most people can do that pretty easily.

Patrick is very interested in the Civil War. He has become an expert on Civil War facts and is always talking about it. It doesn't matter to Patrick who he is with or what their level of interest in this topic is. When other kids try to talk with Patrick about anything else, he continues to talk about the Civil War, which prevents him from connecting with other people. Patrick misses opportunities to make friends, pushing people away by not giving them a chance to talk about what interests them. For Patrick, talking about his favorite topic helps him feel safe and relaxed. When he has to attend to a different topic, Patrick feels anxious and lost. Going back to talking about the Civil War is always a relief to him. Patrick is stuck.

Here's what Patrick needs to know: he can think about, read about, and watch movies about the Civil War at certain times, either when he's with people who are also interested or when he is alone. The only way he will become more comfortable when different topics come up is to practice being part of those conversations.

directions

Do you get stuck?   ☐ Yes ☐ No

If you answered yes, describe how and what you get stuck on:

_____

_____

_____

If you answered no, ask adults who know you well (your parent, counselor, or a family friend) if they think you get stuck, and how. If so, have them give you some examples.

When you are asked to stop thinking or talking about your topic of interest, or when you are asked to change a plan, how do you feel? Create a drawing, collage, poem, or story about this feeling.

take note

Being aware that you are stuck is the first step in learning how to get unstuck. It can be difficult to do on your own. You may need people you trust to help you notice when you are getting stuck. They can just tell you that you're stuck, or together you can come up with a code word or gesture that means "You are stuck" so that they can let you know without having to actually say it.

What code word or gesture do you think would work for you?

_____

Once someone says the code word or uses the gesture, your job is to work on getting unstuck. Using cool-down tools works for some people, helping them to relax enough to try new behaviors. The next activity will give you some suggestions on getting unstuck.

36 how to get unstuck

you need to know

Having the ability to get unstuck when you are with other people will make it easier for you to focus on them. It is a key skill for building friendships.

Farmer Bill has a wheelbarrow that he uses to bring seeds down a narrow path to a patch of land at the back of his farm. Since Farmer Bill takes the same path every day to bring the seeds to that patch, his wheelbarrow has created a rut in the ground. Farmer Bill notices that he's getting slower every day. The rut has gotten so deep that it slows the wheelbarrow down and makes it hard to get where he wants to go. He decides to try to push the wheelbarrow down the path next to the rut and finds that the wheel gets drawn down into the same old rut. It's hard and frustrating for Farmer Bill to create new paths, and he has to work very hard to focus on keeping the wheelbarrow from getting stuck in the old rut.

Thoughts that you might be stuck on can create "ruts" in your thinking that can be compared to habits. To get unstuck, it's necessary to create new paths, which involves becoming aware of those ruts and avoiding them time and time again. That can be difficult, so it's a good idea to keep in mind your ultimate goals of making friends and becoming more comfortable with other people while you go through the process of getting unstuck.

Here are some ideas that may help you get unstuck:

- Be aware of times when you may be getting stuck and say to yourself, "I am stuck."

- Imagine a picture of something getting unstuck, like the wheelbarrow in our example. Draw a picture or an icon that shows how you imagine getting unstuck.

- Use your picture or icon to help you get unstuck. Remember it whenever you think you might be stuck or when someone tells you that you are stuck.

directions

Draw your image of "unstuck" here.

After you draw your image, make a copy of it to keep in your pocket or your backpack as a reminder to pay attention to when you are stuck and to remember how to get unstuck.

take note

Learning how to become unstuck can be difficult, and it can take lots of time and practice. Many people become stuck because they are nervous, and they may not even know why. Practicing the cool-down tools that worked for you and paying attention to your feelings, as well as using your image, will help you.

Just as Farmer Bill, in the example above, needed patience to create a new pathway, so do you. You are actually helping your brain to work in a different way, a way that will help you get unstuck and make it easier for you to have friends. It can take time.

Has anyone ever referred to you as a black-and-white thinker? When you are trying to solve a problem, if you come up with only two possible solutions, you are probably a black-and-white thinker. Often these solutions are all-or-nothing responses, such as, "It's my way or the highway." People who don't get stuck in black-and-white thinking can see shades of gray, giving them a larger range of solutions and more options.

Pete's history assignment is to do a project with three other kids—Maria, Lucy, and Don. This project is the biggest of the year, counting for a large portion of the grade for this class. When the group meets for the first time, they all have great, but different, ideas about how to do the project. As they discuss their ideas, Maria, Lucy, and Don are able to choose a plan that the three of them can live with, but Pete is unable to agree with their decision. He is sure that his ideas are the best and refuses to consider any others. Pete tells the teacher that he wants to do the project his way—the best way—and asks for permission to work alone. The teacher tells Pete he has to work in the group or he will get no credit for the project.

Pete has a problem. In the past, Pete's reaction in a group when he couldn't get others to see things his way had been to leave, refusing to participate. If he leaves this time, his history grade will be unacceptable to him. Because Pete is a black-and-white thinker, he's seeing only two options: the group does it his way, or he refuses to participate. He needs to learn to think in shades of gray or he won't be able to do this project.

directions

The opposite ends of this scale show Pete's black-and-white thinking.

I have the best idea
and you have to do it my way.

I won't participate with you
because you won't do it my way.

Now, look at the following shades-of-gray thinking:

1. Since the teacher is making me do this project with my classmates, I will show up to work with them, but I won't do much to help.

2. If I act as if I respect my classmates' ideas, maybe I will have a better chance of convincing them to do it my way.

3. If I respect my classmates' ideas, maybe they will respect mine.

4. I can do the project with the group, but it may not be as good as if I did it alone.

5. I can see that Maria, Lucy, and Don have ideas different from mine, but their ideas may be good.

6. Working together on this project is important if I want to get along with my classmates and have them respect my ideas.

Are there other shades-of-gray thoughts you can add to this list? Write them here:

_____

_____

_____

_____

_____

_____

Pete now has at least six options because he was able to think in shades of gray. What do you think would be the result of his following through with each option? List your answers:

1. _____

   _____

2. _____

   _____

3. _____

   _____

4. _____

   _____

5. _____

   _____

6. _____

   _____

take note

With practice, our brains are able to shift from black-and-white thinking to shades-of-gray thinking. It is like learning to play tennis; to play well, you have to practice using your arm and shoulder muscles in a new way over and over again. To help you practice thinking in shades of gray, think about a time when your response to someone else was "my way or nothing." Write down your black-and-white thoughts and other details about what happened:

_____

_____

_____

Now, think of six other possible responses you could have had. This might take some time, but as your brain is trained to think in this way, the answers will come to you more quickly.

1. _____

_____

2. _____

_____

3. _____

_____

4. _____

_____

5. _____

_____

6. _____

_____

choosing what to wear 38

you need to know

How you dress—the style, appropriateness, and cleanliness of what you wear—gives other people messages about you that may or may not be true. It's important to learn how to dress in different situations so that you will be looked at in a positive light. It comes naturally to some people; for others, it's a struggle.

For some people, the feel of clothes (waistbands, tags, seams, and textures) becomes the main focus of how they dress. For instance, since Dylan was little, he hated the feel of the waistbands on most pants so he wore sweatpants most of the time. When he was younger, lots of kids wore sweatpants to school. By the time he was in middle school, no one else wore them, except in gym class. It took awhile for Dylan to realize that some of the kids were teasing him because of the way he dressed. He knew that sweatpants were allowed by the school dress code, so he was confused. He wasn't sure how he could tolerate wearing pants with a tighter waistband, but he didn't want to be teased anymore. His mother helped him pick out jeans that were soft. Dylan then practiced wearing them at home for short periods of time to get used to them. He was surprised to find that it took very little time for him to become comfortable with them and wear them all day.

Was it necessary for Dylan to dress to fit in? Some people would argue that how others view you should not be the motivation for how you choose to dress, but in Dylan's case, he did not want to draw extra negative attention to himself. He evaluated the social cost of wearing sweats to school, and he realized he wanted to dress more like the people around him. When Dylan went to get a job, he was told he couldn't wear sweats. He had no choice, and he was lucky enough to have already made the transition to wearing jeans. Learning how to be flexible in the way you dress can help you adapt to many different life situations.

How do you choose clothing based on who you are and the situation you are in so that you can feel true to yourself? Some people use clothing as an identity statement. Others dress for comfort or convenience and don't think about the social aspect. But people do judge you on first impressions, so considering how you look to others can be important. Weighing all these factors can be confusing. The activity below is designed to help you understand what clothing might mean in different settings.

directions

To sharpen your awareness about how people dress in different settings, observe how people look in the following places: school, a business office, a grocery store (both employees and customers), a place of worship, and home.

Now think about yourself and fill in the table below. If you need help figuring out what impression your clothing gives to other people, ask an adult you trust for help.

What I Like To Wear	Setting	Others' Impression of How I Look
Sweats	School	Lazy, ready for bed, "loser"
	Work	Doesn't care about this job
	Home	Perfectly fine
	School	
	Work	
	Home	
	School	
	Work	
	Home	
	School	
	Work	
	Home	
	School	
	Work	
	Home	
	School	
	Work	
	Home	

take note

Now that you have considered how people see you in different settings, the next step is to develop your personal style. You need to weigh the factors of comfort and convenience along with the image you project in a particular setting. Some people find it helpful to take along a trusted person when they shop so they can get feedback on how certain clothes look on them.

After doing this activity, is there anything you want to change about the way you dress? If so, list your ideas here:

_____

_____

_____

_____

_____

Look at your list above. What changes do you feel comfortable making by yourself? What changes might you need help making? Whom can you ask for help?

_____

_____

_____

_____

_____

_____

you need to know

It's important to spend some time thinking about the progress you've made and the things you may still need to work on. By completing this book, you've taken an important step toward social success.

When Jerome looked back at his list of strengths and weaknesses earlier in this book, he realized that one of his weaknesses was being too strict about the rules while playing a game. After doing the activities in this book, Jerome worked on paying attention to when he was choosing rules over friendship. By doing that, Jerome was able to focus on friendship when he became anxious about rules. He found that by taking deep breaths he could keep his thoughts about rules to himself. As a result of this change, Jerome found being around other kids easier, and he noticed that other kids were including him more. Jerome was very happy to see that he had successfully worked on this weakness.

directions

Look back at activity 10 to see what you listed as your strengths and weaknesses when you began this book. List any changes below. If you have trouble thinking about these changes, please ask a trusted person to help you. That person might see new areas you've successfully worked on that may be hard for you to see.

_____

_____

_____

_____

_____

_____

_____

_____

_____

_____

_____

_____

_____

_____

_____

_____

_____

_____

_____

take note

How do you feel about the changes you see in yourself?

_____

_____

_____

_____

_____

_____

_____

_____

Do you think others see these changes? Why?

_____

_____

_____

_____

_____

_____

_____

_____

40 what's next?

you need to know

Now that you have come to the end of this book, it's a good idea for you to think about your strengths and weaknesses again. That way, you can see how far you've come.

Improving your social skills by understanding yourself and the world around you is a challenge. We know from working with lots of kids that change takes time and can be frustrating—and also rewarding! Growth is a lifelong process, and there's always more to learn.

To review, here are some of the skills you worked on by using this book:

- Getting better at knowing what you're feeling

- Understanding yourself and how you think

- Getting better at communicating what you're feeling

- Getting better at understanding what other people are feeling

- Getting better at dealing with disagreements

- Tolerating frustration better, with yourself or other people

- Cooling down when you are anxious or upset

- Making conversation with one other person

- Starting a conversation

- Listening to others

- Making conversation in a group

- Dealing with disagreements with friends

- Being a team player rather than having to be the boss

- Dealing with game rules

- Changing your negative thoughts

- Developing a filter

- Understanding unwritten rules

- Being more flexible in your thinking and behavior

directions

To help you know how much progress you've made, write down your thoughts about the following:

Here are some things I learned from this workbook that have helped me:

_____

_____

_____

_____

_____

_____

_____

_____

Here are some things I still need to work on:

_____

_____

_____

_____

_____

_____

_____

_____

Barbara Cooper, MPS, ATR-BC, LMHC, is a registered, board-certified art therapist with twenty-three years of experience treating children and adults in school, hospital, and private practice settings. Her specialty is helping parents develop their own style of effective parenting. With Widdows, she is codirector of SuperKids, a social skills program in Connecticut. Cooper received her master's degree in art therapy from the Pratt Institute in New York, where she is now an associate professor.

Nancy Widdows, MS, ATR-BC, LPC, is a licensed professional counselor and registered, board-certified art therapist with thirteen years' experience treating children in school, hospital, and private practice settings. Widdows' specialty is using art therapy to create concrete visual tools to help kids understand the social environment. Cooper and Widdows codirect SuperKids, a unique program that focuses exclusively on social skills development, in Ridgefield, Norwalk, and Orange, Connecticut.

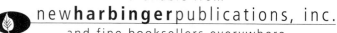

Drug Education

for children aged 4–11

GO\G £4.9.9 98

AF̄ Term-time on̄ hours:

a quick guide

Janice Slough

Folens

Series Advisers

Gerald Haigh   Writer and Consultant in Education

Pauline Maskell   Secondary Head of Health Studies

John Sutton   General Secretary, Secondary Heads Association

Advisory Panel

Ruth Joyce   Adviser on Drugs and Health Education

Mike Kirby   Writer on Education

Terry Saunders   Secondary Head of Biology

Anne Morgan   Primary Deputy Headteacher

Elaine Wilson   Secondary Head of Science

Second edition

ISBN: 1 85467 326 2

© Janice Slough 1995, 1996

Folens Publishers
Albert House
Apex Business Centre
Boscombe Road
Dunstable LU5 4RL
Tel: 01582 472788   Fax: 01582 472575
Printed in Great Britain